THE HUMONGOUS "GOOBER SLICK!"

Story & Illustrations by Carol Ann Conlin

Written with love for my Grandchildren

ISBN: Softcover   978-1-5035-7647-6
        Hardcover   978-1-5035-7648-3
        EBook   978-1-5035-7646-9

Print information available on the last page

Rev. date: 06/05/2015

To order additional copies of this book, contact:
Xlibris
1-888-795-4274
www.Xlibris.com
Orders@Xlibris.com

The Humongous "Goober Slick!"

What's that ringing in my ears?

"Ring, Ring, Ring,"

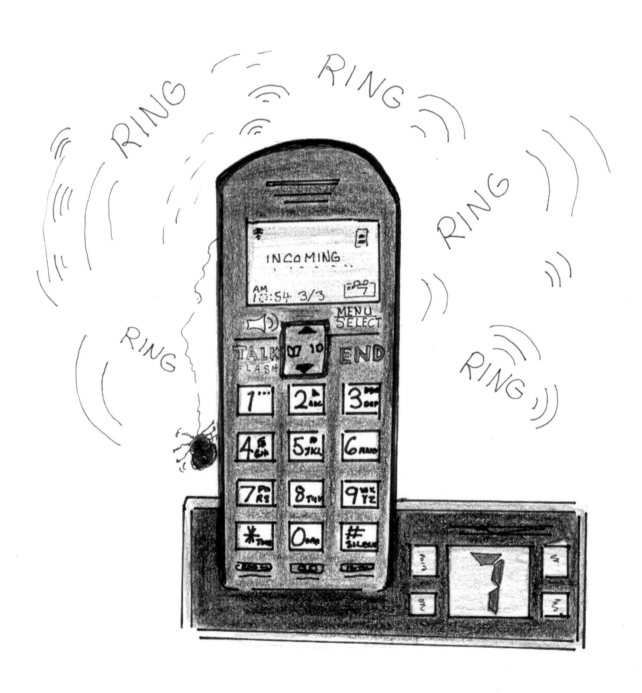

I withdraw to linger on that noisy **"tingler"**.

"Slurp, slurp, slurp!,"

What's that sound?

The evidence is clear to see!

A Humongous "Goober Slick"

is running **d**

o

w

n my cup of tea.

Loudly I declare,

"THAT'S NOT MY CUP OF TEA!"

Then, a tail goes **d**

o

w

n, without a sound,

a head goes **d**

o

w

n, into a frown,

and you go **d**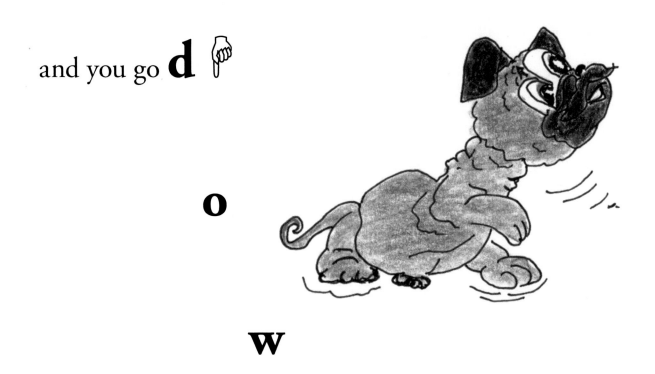

o

w

n, to the ground.

P I spied upon the shelf, a new cup for myself.

U

I poured another cup of tea.

Then I settle back into my favorite space.

Now, with my book in hand, I find my place.

You rest your head upon my knee.

P at me.

You look **U**

Your blue sable seal puppy eyes look so sad!

I pat your little wrinkled head.

It's all you need from me I see.

p, and wags at me.

Your tail goes **u**

p, as if to hear.

Your ears go **u**

Is that a grin, or is it a sneer?

p you go.

Then, **u**

d

o

w

n goes the tea,

d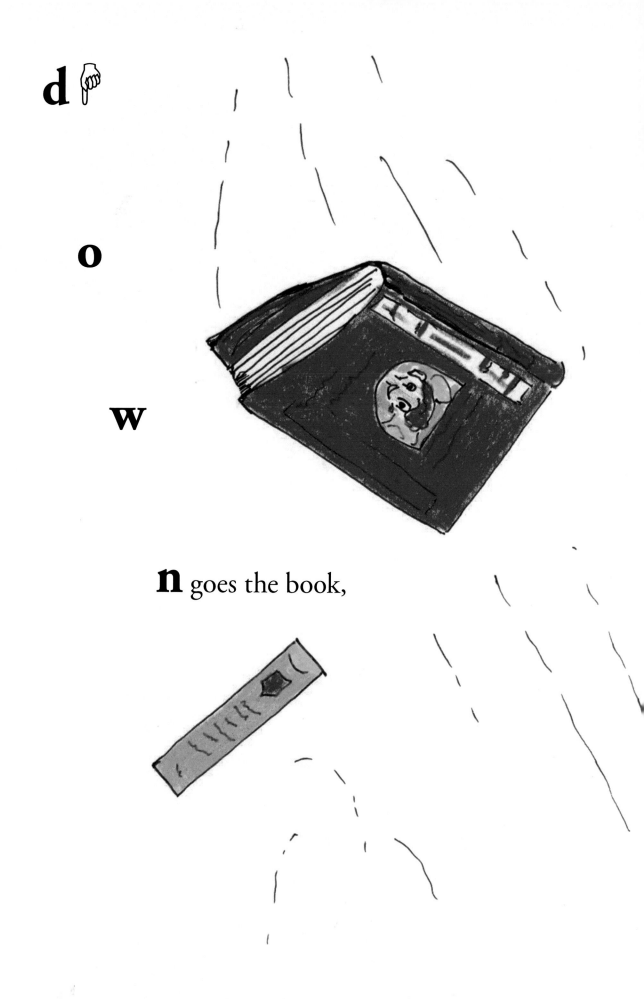

o

w

n goes the book,

and **d**

o

w

n goes me!

15

Here are some pictures of Pugs.

Here is a mother pug and her puppies.

This puppy is 3 days old!

This puppy is three weeks old.

This Pug is wearing a Santa hat!

Happy 1st Birthday Mattie!

This is a Pug/Sharpie.

This is Mattie and Bruce.
They are 3 years old.

Pugs have lots and lots of wrinkles.

Some Pugs have very long tongues.

Here are two photos of Pugs.
Mattie & Bruce.

You can, draw or color a picture of your favorite animal or pet here.

Here is a picture for you to color.

A special thank you to all those who helped
in making this book and to Paul Lieshman
for contributing these two photos.

"Thank you all very much."

Printed in the United States
By Bookmasters